Ready for SCHOOL activities

3-5 YEARS

Illustrated by
Jim Peacock

Designed and produced by
Autumn Publishing Ltd
Chichester, West Sussex

© 2002 Autumn Publishing Ltd

Printed in Spain

ISBN 1 85997 658 1

BYEWAY
BOOKS

Singing in the rain

Starting with the letter 'a', draw a line to join the dots and complete the picture.

Rabbit racer

Starting with the letter 'a', draw a line to join the dots
and complete the picture.

Alphabet

Name each object. Trace the letters.

apple bear Carrot dragon

egg fish gorilla

hat igloo jug

kite lion mouse

 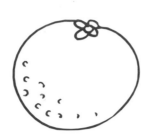  

Nest   Orange   Pear   Queen

Rabbit   Snake   tree

 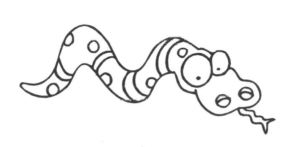 

Umbrella   Violin   Windmill

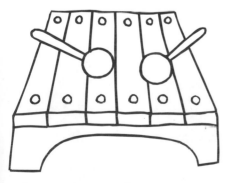  

Xylophone   Yo-yo   Zebra

First letter blocks

Draw lines to match the first letter of each word with the same letters on the blocks.

a b c d e f g h i j k l m

lizards

mittens

stars

bees

cheese

king

feathers

donkey

seal

goat

pirate

treasure

Pick a letter

Draw lines to match the missing letters with each of these words.
Write the letters in the spaces.

house

_alloons

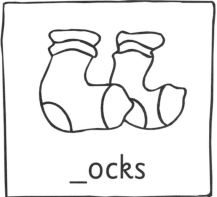

_ocks

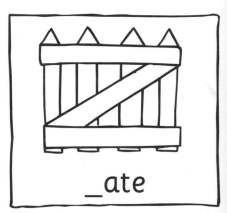

_ate

_nchor

_angaroo

_itch

_ractor

h
a
b
k
s
g
t
w

Pick two letters

Draw lines to match the missing pairs of letters with each of these words.
Write the letters in the spaces.

cl   tr   sc   ch   sn   fl   sw   sh

_ _ _eep

_ _ _eese

_ _ouds

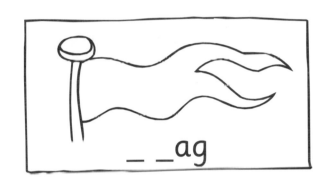

_ _ _ag

_ _ing

_ _ _ain

_ _arecrow

_ _ _ail

Park puzzle

swing

tree

duck

see-saw

bicycle

ED'S ICES

Look at the words around the page. Can you find these things in this picture? Draw lines to join the words with the picture.

boy

dog

girl

swan

roundabout

ice cream

flower

At home

bed

window

boat

box

pillow

poster

teddy bear

Colour the picture. Look at the words around the page.
Can you find these things in this picture?
Draw lines to join the words with the picture.

pencil

doll

book

rug

table

curtains

pyjamas

rabbit

Animal magic

Choose a letter to complete the words.

c
d
r

_og

_at

_abbit

g
l
e

_lephant

_iraffe

_ion

p
c
g

_ow

_ig

_oat

Complete the words

Choose the correct letter to complete the words.

s		m
_un		

x		m
_oon		

t		s
_tars		

c		t
_hair		

w		d
_oor		

s		b
_ink		

n		c
_ar		

r		b
_us		

v		l
_orry		

Rhyme-time picnic

Colour the picture.
Draw lines to join the words that rhyme.

loose

jelly

toast

cake

pear

runny

stare

Opposites

Point to the words on this page and find their opposites on the next page.

closed

dirty

thin

empty

day

short

How are they feeling?

Complete the words to describe how these children are feeling.

_appy

_ngry

_ad

_ _ared

_ired

Hidden words

Cross out the letters that appear twice in each grid
to reveal two hidden words.

b	r	o	s
c	d	c	r
a	e	s	d
w	e	t	w

f	b	t	o
x	u	i	r
r	t	u	b
s	o	x	h

Capital letters

Names begin with a capital letter. Trace the capital letters of these names.
Can you spot the twins?

Ace   Boris   Colin

Dotty   Ethel   Felix

Gert   Herbert   Incy

Java   Kissy   Lurch   Mindy

Nessy

Ollie

Percy

Queenie

Rusty

Sassy

Tubby

Um

Vernon

Wally

Xerox

Yeti

Zig

Party time

Who would you invite to a party?
Fill in the missing words.

Dear _____,

I am having a party

on _____

at _____.

I will be _____ years old.

I hope you can come.

From _____

Party list

Complete this list of things for your party.

Things to buy:

_ats

ball_ _ns

_ames

_ _esents

Food:

pi_ _a

_ _isps

sandwi_ _es

ca_e

Which sign?

Look at the signs around the page.
Fill in the missing words in the picture.

TOYS

OPEN

CAR PARK

DANGER

Colour and shape mice

Trace the words in the shapes.
Colour this picture using the key in the box. How many of each shape can you count?

triangle

circle

square

rectangle

KEY

triangles	–	red
circles	–	blue
squares	–	green
rectangles	–	yellow
diamonds	–	purple
stars	–	orange
ovals	–	pink

oval

star

diamond

Gerald giraffe

Copy the number words from one to ten.

10 ten _____

9

8 eight _____

nine _____

7

seven _____

6

six _____

five _____

5

4 four _____

three _____

3

2 two _____

one _____

1

Numbers 1 to 10

Count the objects and complete the number words.

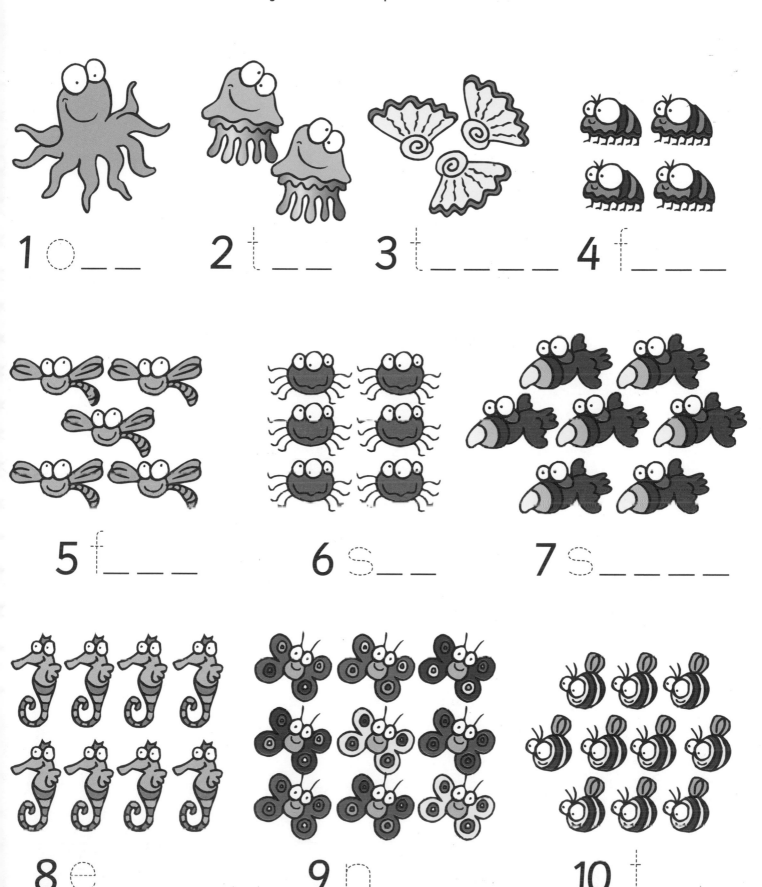

1 o _ _

2 t _ _

3 t _ _ _ _

4 f _ _ _

5 f _ _ _

6 s _ _

7 s _ _ _ _ _

8 e _ _ _ _ _

9 n _ _ _

10 t _ _

Counting bugs

How many bugs can you see in the picture?
To help you count, colour each type of bug in a different colour.
Write your answers in the boxes.

snails	worms	ladybirds	butterflies

bees
spiders
ants
beetles

Cool cats

How many different cats can you see in the picture?

black cats	ginger cats	white cats

cats with
blue stripes

brown cats

cats with
sunglasses

Wishing well

Starting with number 1, draw a line to join the dots and complete the picture.

Cows in space

Starting with number 1, draw a line to join the dots and complete the picture.

Maze magic

Follow the numbers from 1 to 10 to help this wizard through the maze to the crystal ball.

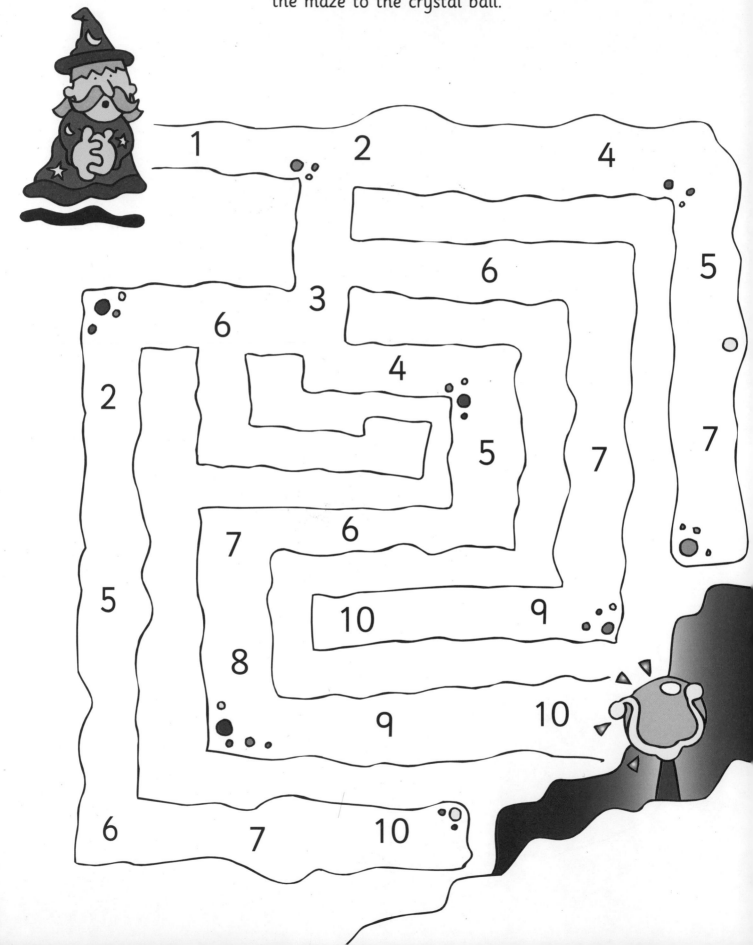

The most toadstools

Which fairy has the most toadstools?
Draw a circle around her.

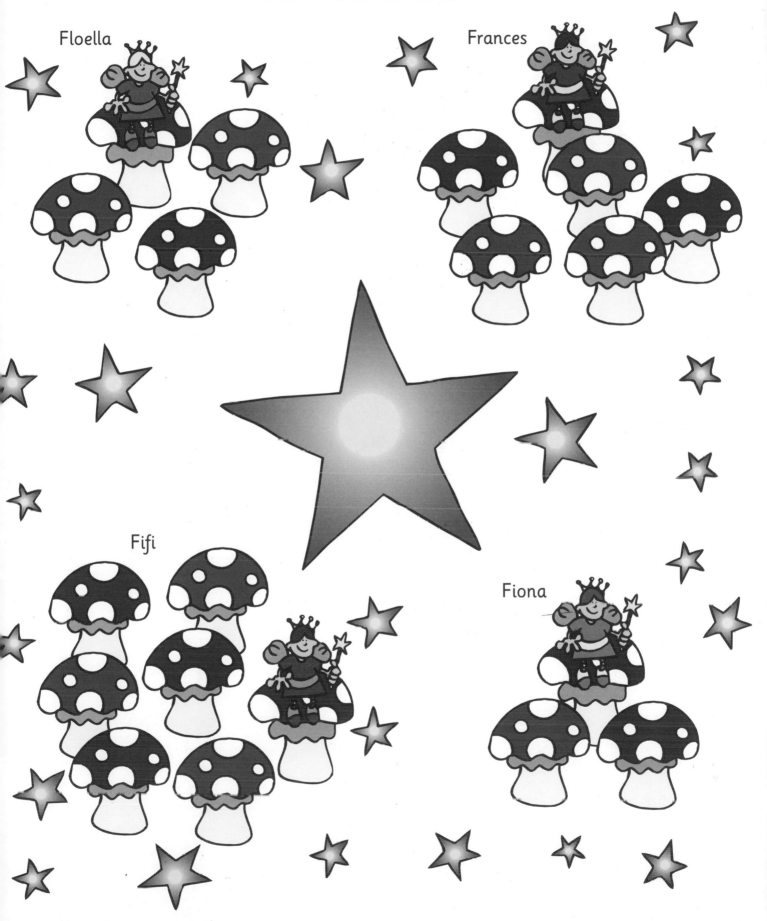

Floella

Frances

Fifi

Fiona

Flower sums

Look at the adding up sums on this page.

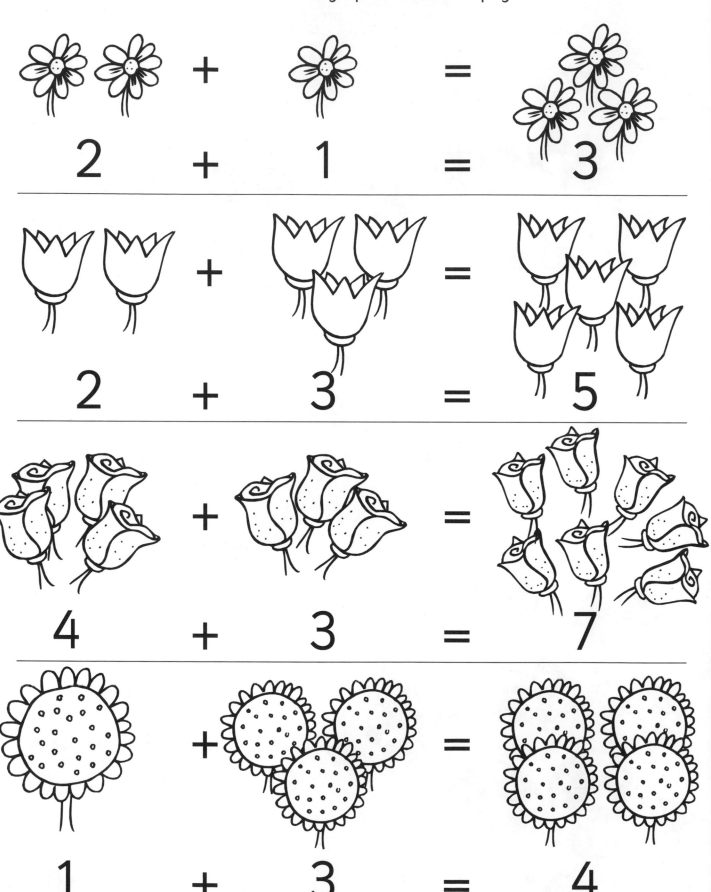

2   +   1   =   3

2   +   3   =   5

4   +   3   =   7

1   +   3   =   4

Garden sums

Now do the adding up sums on this page.

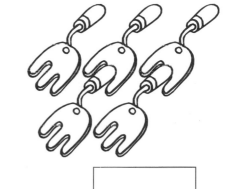

2 + 2 =

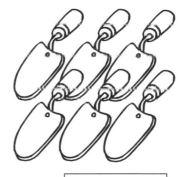

2 + 3 =

3 + 3 =

Do this sum and draw the answer.

3 + 1 =

Stripes and spots

How many stripy zebras are there?

How many spotty leopards are there?

How many stripy snakes are there?

Sea match

Do the sums. Draw lines to match the answers to the
same number of sea creatures.

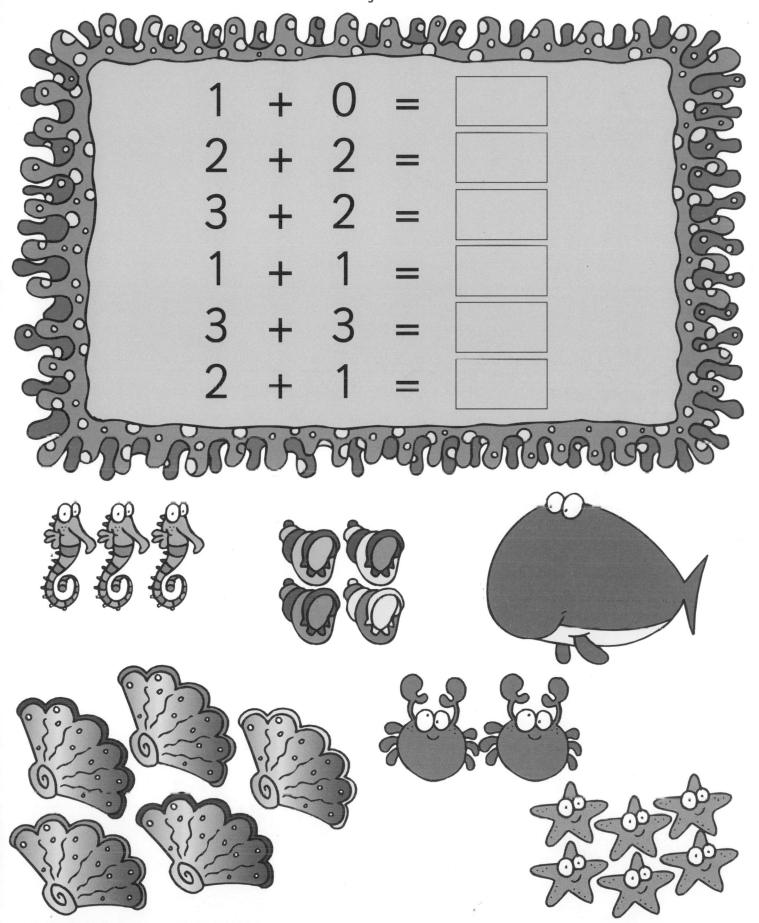

$$1 + 0 = \boxed{}$$
$$2 + 2 = \boxed{}$$
$$3 + 2 = \boxed{}$$
$$1 + 1 = \boxed{}$$
$$3 + 3 = \boxed{}$$
$$2 + 1 = \boxed{}$$

Weather sums

Look at the taking away sums on this page.

2   –   1   =   1

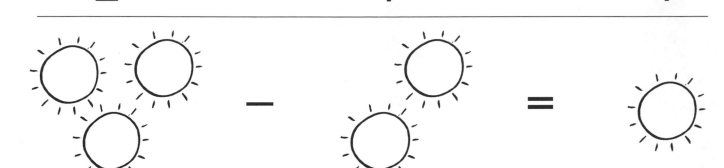

3   –   2   =   1

4   –   2   =   2

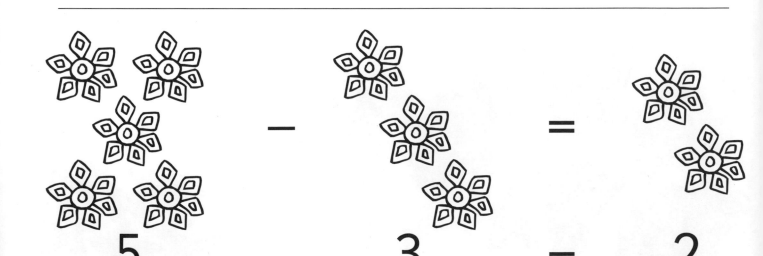

5   –   3   =   2

Space sums

Now do the taking away sums on this page.

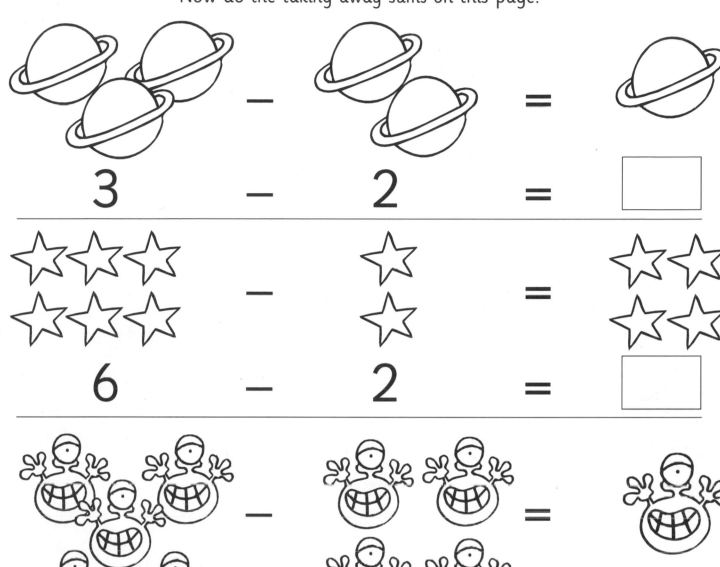

3   –   2   =   ☐

6   –   2   =   ☐

5   –   4   =   ☐

Do this sum and draw the answer.

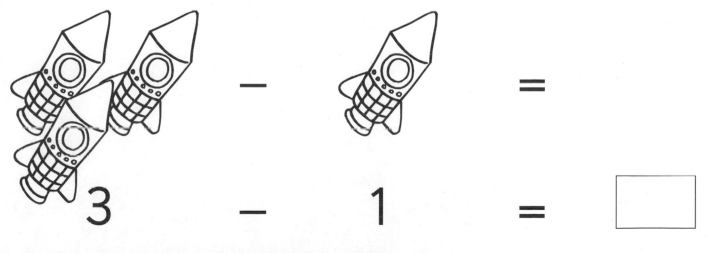

3   –   1   =   ☐

Fred the fruit-seller

Fred has 8 apples. If he sells 4, how many will be left?

8 - 4 = ⬚

Fred has 7 bananas. If he sells 3, how many will be left?

7 - 3 = ⬚

Fred has 8 oranges. If he sells 7, how many will be left?

8 - [ ] = [ ]

Fred has 9 pears. If he sells 6, how many will be left?

[ ] - [ ] = [ ]

Answers

Pick a letter
<u>h</u>ouse <u>b</u>alloons <u>s</u>ocks <u>g</u>ate
<u>a</u>nchor <u>k</u>angaroo <u>w</u>itch <u>t</u>ractor

Pick two letters
<u>sh</u>eep <u>ch</u>eese <u>cl</u>ouds <u>fl</u>ag
<u>sw</u>ing <u>tr</u>ain <u>sc</u>arecrow <u>sn</u>ail

Animal magic
<u>d</u>og <u>c</u>at <u>r</u>abbit
<u>e</u>lephant <u>g</u>iraffe <u>l</u>ion
<u>c</u>ow <u>p</u>ig <u>g</u>oat

Complete the words
<u>s</u>un <u>m</u>oon <u>st</u>ars
<u>ch</u>air <u>d</u>oor <u>s</u>ink
<u>c</u>ar <u>b</u>us <u>l</u>orry

Rhyme-time picnic
jelly - smelly   toast - most
cake - make   pear - stare
juice - loose   honey - runny

Opposites
night - day   long - short
full - empty   open - closed
clean - dirty   fat - thin

How are they feeling?
<u>h</u>appy <u>a</u>ngry <u>s</u>ad <u>sc</u>ared <u>t</u>ired

Hidden words
boat fish

Capital letters
Dotty and Ollie are the twins.

Party list
<u>h</u>ats   <u>p</u>izza
<u>b</u>alloons   <u>cr</u>isps
<u>g</u>ames   <u>s</u>andwiches
<u>p</u>resents   <u>c</u>ake

Colour and shape mice
triangles -	3	diamonds -	2
circles -	3	stars -	3
squares -	3	ovals -	2
rectangles -	3		

Counting bugs
snails -	6	bees -	7
worms -	6	spiders -	6
ladybirds -	5	ants -	6
butterflies -	5	beetles -	4

Cool cats
black cats -	5	brown cats -	7
ginger cats -	4	cats with	
white cats -	2	sunglasses -	6
cats with			
blue stripes -	3		

The most toadstools
Fifi has the most toadstools.

Garden sums
$2 + 2 = 4$ $2 + 3 = 5$
$3 + 3 = 6$ $3 + 1 = 4$

Sea match
$1 + 0 = 1$ $2 + 2 = 4$
$3 + 2 = 5$ $1 + 1 = 2$
$3 + 3 = 6$ $2 + 1 = 3$

Stripes and spots
zebras - 4
leopards - 4
snakes - 7

Space sums
$3 - 2 = 1$ $6 - 2 = 4$
$5 - 4 = 1$ $3 - 1 = 2$

Fred the fruit-seller
$8 - 4 = 4$ $8 - 7 = 1$
$7 - 3 = 4$ $9 - 6 = 3$